Did You Ever Think These Would Be In The Trees?

By Wendy Starkey

Not again! Another year? All this snow makes tree eyes tear!

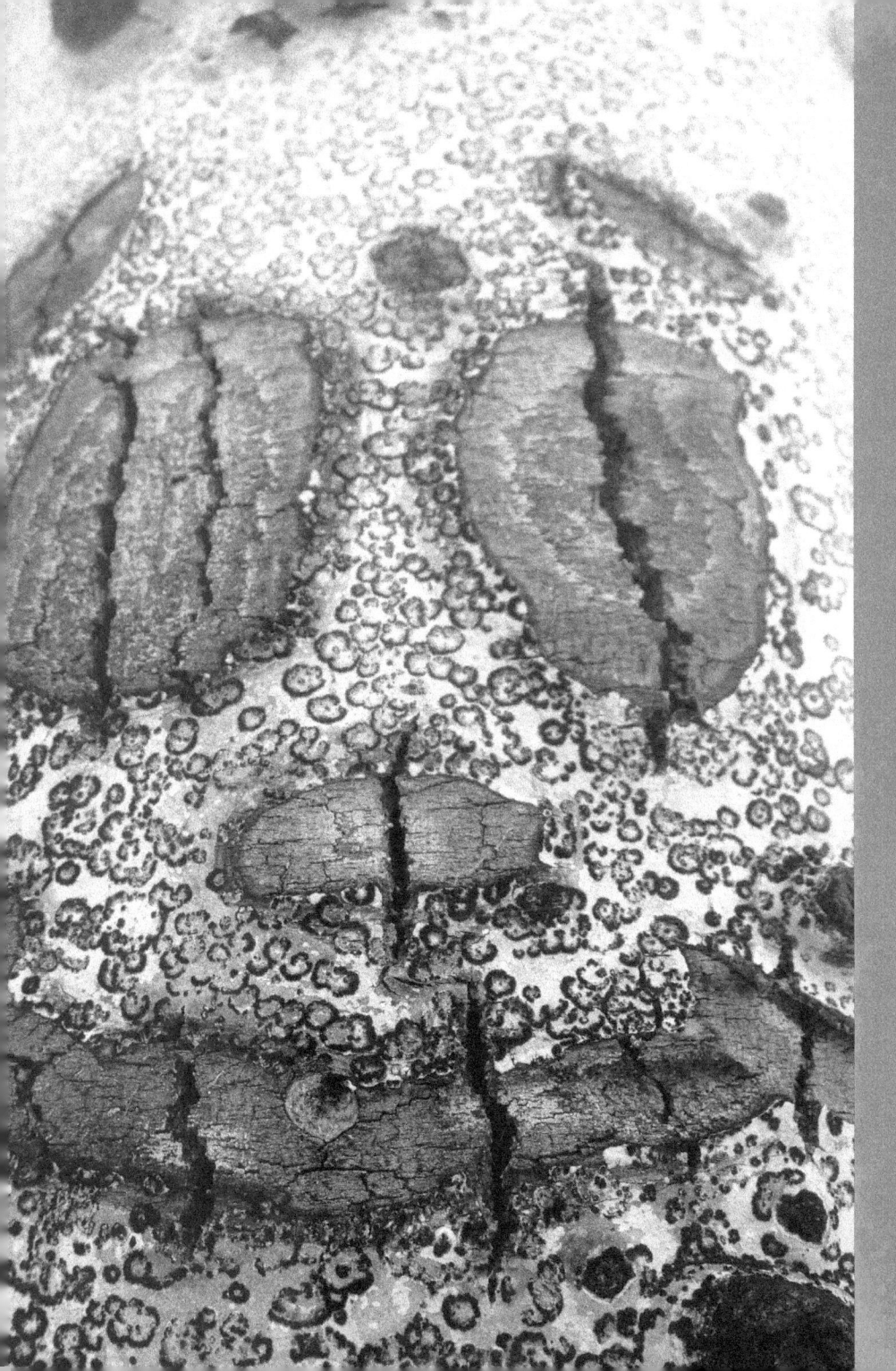

Can you see me?
I can see you!
Cracking this smile
wasn't easy to do.

Quietly hiding, this little hedgehog is easily missed when attached to a log.

Sit up in a tree and enjoy the view. What else would a winter snow woman do?

You might be tired from hiking long miles; I know you'll feel better just seeing tree smiles!

Don't be afraid when I come into sight. I'll stick out my tongue, but I really won't bite.

Trees are so smart. They know their numbers! They show us their art from peaceful slumbers!

You may need to ask, "Is it buck or a doe?" I can't explain, because only trees know!

Slinking, sleeping, hissing, or tied? Tangled up roots show what is inside.

Scaling up on mushroom feet, life in the trees just can't be beat!

They say that elephants never forget! Well, neither do trees I'm willing to bet.

Let out a scream if you're really afraid! My branches are gone; I can't give you shade.

Aren't these sightings just such a hoot? Now where is the cowboy who's missing his boot?

Every day I sit and stare, but at least I've got some groovy hair.

King of the beasts, in silent gaze. Looks to the east, counting the days.

Wanting to see around the curve, a tree can just grow its trunk in a swerve.

A giant stands guard at the edge of this wood. I want to keep hiking, do you think I should?

Wiggly and squiggly,
wispy, and quick,
this bug looks so real
etched into a stick.

I'm out on the playground, where the cold wind blows. I'll watch you have fun with two eyes and a nose.

Trying to travel high up a trunk, a spider that big could eat a chipmunk!

So now I can prove that trees DO feel LOVE! They quietly show us from branches above.

Now share this with friends or whomever you please. I Would never think "These" would be in the trees?!

Author Wendy Starkey is an Educator and outdoor enthusiast. She truly believes that more outdoor play and family time will help develop today's children into more empathetic, kind, and responsible human beings. Living in the Tetons, Mrs. Starkey hikes, skis, or rides her horses in some of the nation's most beautiful places. Connecting our youth with the earth and with reading will strengthen their imaginations and build memories. So out you go people, go read in the trees!

www.ingramcontent.com/pod-product-compliance
Lightning Source LLC
LaVergne TN
LVHW081528060526
838200LV00045B/2045

9780578603049